IMAGES OF ENGLAND

YORK PEOPLE
1850–1980

IMAGES OF ENGLAND

YORK PEOPLE
1850–1980

YVETTE TURNBULL

TEMPUS

This book is respectfully dedicated to the staff of York Libraries, who made my time with them the happiest of my working life.

Frontispiece: The exact function of these gloriously uniformed buglers is unknown, although obviously ceremonial. The mysteries surrounding them are legion although the photograph is thought to date from around 1890.

First published 2005

Tempus Publishing Limited
The Mill, Brimscombe Port,
Stroud, Gloucestershire, GL5 2QG
www.tempus-publishing.com

© Yvette Turnbull, 2005

The right of Yvette Turnbull to be identified as the Author
of this work has been asserted in accordance with the
Copyrights, Designs and Patents Act 1988.

British Library Cataloguing in Publication Data.
A catalogue record for this book is available from the British Library.

ISBN 0 7524 3716 X

Typesetting and origination by Tempus Publishing Limited.
Printed in Great Britain.

Contents

Acknowledgements 6

Introduction 7

one Home and Play 9

two Work and School 37

three War and Peace 59

four Worship and Celebration 75

five Out and About 99

Acknowledgements

The images for this book and their accompanying research have been taken from the Imagine York website, which was created by a group of erudite and passionately committed volunteers, a fiercely enthusiastic project board and me, the project officer, with the support of the best project assistants I could have dreamt of. Working on this book using the site as a resource has been such a pleasure and everyone deserves to be named once more:

Volunteers: Jane Burrows, David Hodgin, the late Geoff Hodgson, Peter A. Jackson, Joe Murphy, Anne Paver, David Poole, Jill Shuttleworth, Wendy Simmons, John Terry and Helen Travis.

Project Board: Maia Daguerre, Rita Freedman, Julie Grant, Sue Richmond, Sue Rigby and Janet Thompson.

Project Assistants: Nicky Copley, Edward Freedman, Bev Muse, Isobel Walker.

The kindergarten of New Earswick School are pictured at lunchtime, *c.* 1917. The teachers are thought to be Miss Pritchard and Miss Ashford. The Village Trust had been providing a temporary infant school in the Folk Hall from 1908 but it wasn't until 1910 that an arrangement was made with the Education Authority for appropriate provision.

Introduction

There is something mesmerising about looking into the eyes of a person in an old photograph. What have those eyes seen? As Roland Barthes said of an 1852 photograph of Napoleon's brother: 'I realized then, with an amazement I have not been able to lessen since: "I am looking at eyes that looked at the Emperor".' For me this has always been one of the fascinations of the work I have done with the collection of historic photographs which is held by the City of York libraries and archives service. The people. The eyes of the people. What have their experiences been? What have they understood of life? If I had met them, and talked with them, would we have found any common ground at all? I worked on an autograph book belonging to a young Edwardian woman who lived in a pleasant house in Strensall. She asked her friends to sign her book and they wrote little poems and comments with their name and the date. Many were young men. She added photographs, cuttings, little scraps about daily life. And later? Later she added the dates and the battles in which they died during the bloody horror of the First World War. I held her scrapbook, and I touched the photographs, and in some way felt that I had some connection to her as she wrote again and again over the photographs of her friends, of the young men, 'RIP'.

But not all the associations are as sad or as harsh as this. There are the photographs of the people laughing at a gala, the images of the moneyed middle classes dressed in their best clothes enjoying the races, and amongst them the young fruit seller whose eyes are not on her stand but on the race as it is played out beyond the sight of the camera. There are the young groups of friends having fun, feeling free, able to explore more widely outside their usual world because of that exciting invention, the bicycle. There are the posed group photographs of people setting off on their charabanc trip around Buttercrambe Woods – would their excitement and pleasure really be any different from ours as we set off to the airport to enjoy our holiday, or do the traffic jams on the way to the theme park make their experience one to be envied? I look at them and I wonder.

There is the poverty of course. York was full of slums where children grew up with poor sanitation, sharing a room with numberless siblings and there are images showing precisely that – children with dirty faces, rooms with damp walls, women with careworn expressions and ugly clothes. But there are also so many pictures of poor people with carefully polished boots, beautifully pressed clothes and lovingly cared-for homes. There are endless photographs of women scrubbing steps.

For me photographs capture life at a specific time and place. They help me to understand and, in some small way, even to experience a little of the past. In this book I have presented the people and their daily lives – there are photographs of children in school, of people working, glimpses of domestic interiors, snatches of the excitement of high days and holidays when royalty visited or when the great moments of history touched the city.

In the early days of photography people were relatively rare in photographs as proponents of the new art sought acceptance from the wider cultured world.

York Model Band, *c.* 1860. York has a long and glorious history of music making, as it has the longest-established musical society in Europe.

Early photographers not only had the disadvantage inherent in long exposure times but sought to create photographic images which echoed paintings. The reportage style could not appear until after advances in technology allowed the 'snapshot' or candid image to be created – people could actually be caught unawares going about their daily business and did not need to hold their pose for a minute or longer. Even as the technologies advanced many photographers still waited for a scene to clear of people before they took their picture – empty streets and the purity of architecture or the beauty of an unsullied, untouched landscape was what they sought in their composition. Yet these are the pictures that seem less interesting today – certainly one can wonder at the developments in the street and enjoy the changes and similarities to how we know the same place today, but there is nowhere for the imagination to go. We cannot empathise with an empty street. We cannot seek to understand its life for it doesn't have one of its own without the people who inhabit it.

So, I hope that you are able to savour these photographs. To look into the eyes of the people who inhabit its pages and to imagine. To imagine our past and their present. To imagine the York that they inhabited, or to revisit it if it is also part of your past. I hope you can feel the same connection; to look into the eyes that may have looked into the eyes of an Emperor.

one

Home
and Play

This marvellously relaxed young gentleman is thought to be Sheldon, the brother of a Miss Hodgkinson who lived at The Lodge in Strensall and kept an album of photographs, autographs, poems and memorabilia from which this is taken. Sheldon appears in other photographs in her album and was probably a rather less lethargic young man than this picture suggests.

Opposite above: By the time this unknown couple took up their vertiginous position on the roof of the minster (*c.* 1890) photography was a very popular pastime. Cameras were cheaper than they had been even a few years before, and were therefore much more easily available to ordinary people who could use them to record special events or days out like this one.

Opposite below: Riverside living has always given the people of York wonderful opportunities for relaxing and just watching the busy traffic on the Ouse. These Edwardians are pictured near Lendal Bridge, *c.* 1910.

Yearsley Open-air Baths in the River Foss were York's first municipal baths, opened in 1860. The riverbed was cemented for around 100 yards, approximately behind the present Yearsley Crescent. Swimming was free and, since most of the poorer men swam naked, for males only. The facilities were in use up to the 1930s but this picture dates from around 1900.

York's rivers have also provided entertainment in the winter months. These skaters on the Ouse are pictured towards Lendal Bridge from the bank near Scarborough Railway Bridge in around 1900. During the Great Freeze of 1740 Thomas Gent set up his printing press on the river and produced a handbill to celebrate the event.

Above and below: This melee of rafts are some of the entrants in the June 1978 raft race on the River Ouse. The somewhat eccentric nature of the racers is a far cry from the businesslike garb of entrants in the regattas of the 1920s and '30s, and the neatly gymslipped women of previous years shown on later pages may have found this race more than a little startling.

PC Cutt was the winner of the Alderman Inglis Cup for Plain Diving at the York City Police Swimming Sports at Rowntree Park in the mid-1920s. The baths, which opened in July 1924, were open-air and unheated with no admission charges until 1944. Budget cuts forced their closure in 1980 and they were demolished in 1986.

Miss L. Cossins and crew won the Rowntree Challenge Bowl in the Ladies' Fours competition at the regatta in 1928. They were: L. Cossins (stroke), C. Ferguson, B. Rose, P.K. Lickley and M. Lunnis (cox). They beat Miss Bowling and crew by two lengths. The regatta was a yearly event which in 1928 was used to mark the end of Civic Week.

Members of the York Railway Institute Band are playing on the Ouse in June 1978. The band was established in 1883 by a lay preacher and choirmaster called Noah Bruce and since then there has always been a Bruce in the band. The band continues today and is York's oldest brass band.

The alpine glassade (or helter-skelter) owned by R. Holdsworth was one of the attractions on offer at the Yorkshire Gala, held in the grounds of Bootham Hospital. This 1905 picture gives an idea of the large numbers of people who attended the gala every year. It was held annually from 1858 until 1934 and its purpose was threefold – to raise money for local charities, to provide a forum for exhibiting flowers and produce, and to entertain visitors. In 1875 for example, the attractions included a floral fete with prize money of £550, military bands, a 'great bird show', Signor Levene, the Eline Troop of Vaulters, fireworks and Professor Thurlo. Records don't show what the latter's talents consisted of.

Captain Harry Spencer is testing his parachute in preparation for a jump from a balloon as part of the gala during Civic Week in June 1928. The balloon would climb to around 1,000ft, piloted by Percival Spencer, before the Captain would parachute down onto the Knavesmire. The balloon then made a tour of the city. There were three flights – one on each day of the gala. Captain Spencer's planned landing was in front of the stands on the Knavesmire but on one jump he was blown off course and missed his target by some considerable distance, eventually landing near the Bumper Castle pub on Wigginton Road.

This page and following photograph: This large crowd is gathered for an ox-roasting on St George's Field in 1924. This area had long been the site of the hiring fairs where young men and women could go to advertise their availability for work on the land. These fairs were accompanied by stalls and entertainments and later, long after the original purpose was forgotten, the fairs continued as a much-anticipated gathering, often accompanied by a circus. The sign on the left in the photograph on the following page invites the crowd to 'Guess the weight of the ox'. The man with the megaphone is Councillor Watson, who is announcing the price of the sandwiches to the crowd – judging by the expression on some of the women's faces they consider them to be over-priced!

Sanger's Circus on St George's Field, *c.* 1908. George Sanger had begun his circus in a small way in the 1850s, but as his reputation grew he and his brother John not only ran the successful Travelling Circus, but also took over the world famous Astley's Amphitheatre in London. By 1908 'Lord' John Sanger, John's son, was the manager.

The York and Ainsty Hunt is pictured at Poppleton, *c.* 1927. The hounds hunted a massive area – from Thirsk to Selby and from Howden to Pateley Bridge. Captain the Honourable Henry Butler, son of the 11th Viscount Mountgarret, had kept a small pack of foxhounds shortly after Waterloo (in 1815) with a licence to hunt over an elongated north-south area around York.

This earlier picture (from around 1890) shows the meet at Heslington Hall. Sir Charles Slingsby had been Master for seventeen seasons when in 1869 he drowned, along with his kennelsman Charles Orvis, two followers and nine horses when the overloaded Newby ferry overturned. Thirteen men and eleven horses had boarded after the fox swam across the Ouse but Sir Charles' horse, Saltfish, jumped and capsized it.

Above: In addition to hunting, racing has always been important in York – when Severus arrived in the city in AD 208 in order to suppress the rebellion in the north of the country his train included Arabian racehorses. However, finding an area to race around the city had always been difficult as the surroundings were often boggy. In the extremely cold winter of 1607/08 racing had actually been held on the frozen River Ouse. This bookie is pictured in the 1920s in the far more salubrious surroundings of the purpose-built course on the Knavesmire, which was first used for this purpose in 1731 after flooding at Clifton and Clifton Ings made their use impossible.

Opposite: The crowds attending the autumn meetings in 1908 and 1909 are pictured only a few years after it had seemed certain that the races on the Knavesmire would cease. The lease from the Corporation had run out and the new landlords were the pasture-masters, most of whom were disinterested in the racing as their concern was for the cattle on the stray and for the rent that could be extracted from the Race Committee, whom they perceived as privileged and self-indulgent. The Race Committee undertook years of special negotiation which included an Act of Parliament and, by 1907, the Race Committee had achieved sole control of the Knavesmire during race weeks and a thirty-five-year lease.

Even the fruitseller is absorbed by the racing at the Autumn 1905 meet! She is standing in front of the delicate arcading of the County Stand, which was designed by John Carr, master mason, and opened in 1754. Charles Wentworth, the Marquess of Rockingham, had become dissatisfied with the poor amenities at the Knavesmire, where the wealthy watched the races from their carriages, limiting social intercourse between them. The design and construction of the County Stand marked the beginning of a long and most illustrious career for Carr as well as a lifelong friendship for the two men.

Opposite: It is unlikely that these crowds (in 1906 and 1908) were aware of (or cared much about) the long shared history of racing and public executions. Public hangings took place on the York Tyburn on the Knavesmire, with the August meeting following the hangings from the August assizes. As the popularity of the August meeting grew each year so the number of executions increased. The last public hanging on the Tyburn was in 1801 – the first had been in 1379.

Right: There have been many developments since 1908 when this crowd was gathered, such as a massive new stand and the loss of part of the old façade. The lease runs to 2056, although the Knavesmire's vulnerability to flooding makes it unsuitable as a year-round venue.

Below: The Knavesmire is considered one of the greatest racecourses in Europe, although it was a long time between visits from the reigning monarch: a gap of nearly 340 years occurred between Charles I's visit and that of Queen Elizabeth II, who first visited in 1972. Her Majesty is pictured here in May 1974 watching Lester Piggott dismount from Escorial after winning the Musidora Stakes.

Above: The Lawrence Street Cycling Club is seen here in around 1890. At this time York had many cycling clubs and bicycles were seen as a great bringer of freedom for the ordinary person. Members would arrange rides many miles into the countryside, perhaps having lunch in some pleasant country village and enjoying fresh air and exercise with their friends.

Left: This woman is standing in front of 'Higham' on Stockton Lane in Heworth, *c.* 1913. By this time women were cycling almost as much as men, although not so many years earlier the sight of a woman on a bike would have scandalised most observers.

Right: The exact reason for this photograph is unknown but the caps that all the men are wearing suggest that the team is representing the Britannia Inn (on Heworth) in some area of sporting endeavour, *c.* 1925.

Below: The Jockeys' football teams are pictured in around 1922 at the North (black shirts) versus South (white shirts) jockeys' football match. James Melrose, Chair of the Race Committee, is holding the trophy. He was known as 'the grand old man of York', being born in 1828 into a family of fellmongers (sheepskin dealers) and having an illustrious career, including being elected Lord Mayor in 1876.

The South Bank Working Men's Cricket Club are pictured on the Knavesmire in August 1925. The gentleman on the far right is Tom Russell, who was the professional at the Railway Institute Golf Club on Hob Moor. He lived in an old railway carriage, which was also the clubhouse, and his wage was £2 15s 0d.

The women's team, taking part in the annual 'Ladies versus Gentlemen' cricket match at Nether Poppleton, look very serious, which may indicate that they are intent upon winning. It is unclear whether the men in the background are members of the opposing team.

July '13

The exact location of this picture is unknown although it is in the area of George Street in Walmgate and was taken by the Health Department in the 1950s, probably because the houses in this area were considered unsanitary and were candidates for demolition. The yards which such houses backed on to would have contained toilet facilities for several families and were often surrounded by industrial activity, such as tanning, which was responsible for noxious smells. Today though, similar houses within the city walls fetch large prices and are considered most desirable.

Opposite above: A number of social clubs were based at the Folk Hall in New Earswick. It was also used to continue the tradition of adult education to which the Rowntrees were so committed. The societies reflected the interests of the residents, as this picture from around 1915 shows. The hall was built in 1906 and cost £2,278 15s 1½d.

Opposite below: This table of guests are attending a garden party at Kilburn House in Fulford in July 1913. This was the home of Alderman Joseph Agar, the bearded gentleman on the left. He was an alderman for nearly forty years and laid numerous foundation stones. It is reported that when he died he had a collection of over seventy presentation mallets and trowels.

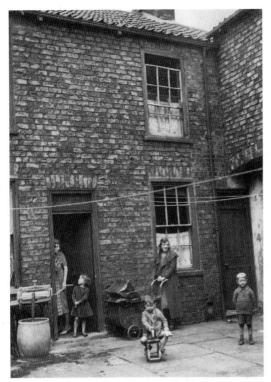

Left: It would be wrong to suggest that life was anything but hard work for women at this time, as in so many ages throughout history. They would have had little or nothing in the way of domestic appliances to help them – note the mangle and dolly tub on the left. This is West Yard (which was off School Street in Walmgate) in 1933.

Below: This is a Corporation photograph, part of a portfolio of pictures collected by the city prior to improvements which were planned within the city centre. These little girls are at the corner of Little Silver Street and Silver Street off Townend Street in May 1957.

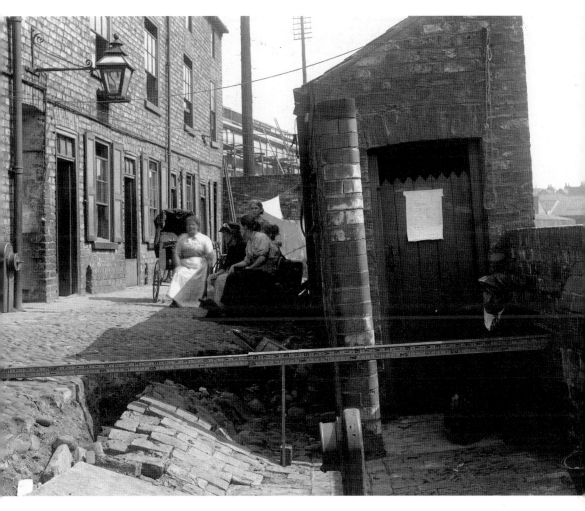

The subsidence on Dennis Street in June 1922 was probably caused by flooding, as the Foss is on the other side of the wall on the right-hand side and was responsible for flooding this area many times. The man is in front of an outdoor lavatory which has a sign reading 'Dangerous not to be used', although the group of women look less than concerned by what is presumably not a little inconvenience. Many houses on this street were demolished in the mid- to late 1930s.

The condition of this house in Walmgate in 1933 was an ample demonstration of the need to improve housing for many residents of the city. This house had been designated a slum – note the mould on the wall – and was due to be demolished. During the 1920s and '30s large numbers of terraced houses were demolished and the residents re-housed in new estates such as Tang Hall, which was begun in 1919 specifically for residents of Walmgate and Hungate.

Opposite above: The nonchalant gentleman leaning on his mantelpiece is thought to be Doctor George Swanson. He lived in Lawrence House on Lawrence Street and owned and ran a private lunatic asylum at this address from around 1875 to around 1898, when he moved to Heworth.

Opposite below: This woman, probably one of the doctor's maids, is also pictured in Lawrence House. The doctor was a keen amateur photographer and almost certainly took this picture himself – a second camera is on the table on the left of the frame.

This very pleasant and homely interior shows the parlour of No. 37 Stonegate in the late 1890s. This was the living quarters of W.F. Greenwood's antique dealers shop, which was established in 1829 in High Ousegate and moved to these premises in 1851 as dealers in 'ancient furniture'. The firm was visited in the first half of the twentieth century by Queen Mary, a notorious 'visitor' of antique shops. Many dealers dreaded her descending upon them, since she had a reputation for 'honouring' proprietors of the finest antique shops by requiring the best items on display to be sent to one of her palaces but never making any payment. Some dealers reputedly resorted to hiding their finest stock when they knew she was visiting the area, for fear of losing it to this most discerning of patrons. It was said that the Queen similarly honoured her hosts when she stayed at private houses, bestowing her praise on the finest pieces and being mortally offended if they were not consequently offered to her as gifts.

two

Work and School

Charles Francis Howell ran a dairy business for many years from Finsbury Street in South Bank. This wonderful woman, probably a member of the Howell family, is pictured delivering milk in the 1920s.

Opposite above: York's first telephone exchange was housed over a chemist's shop in Parliament Street and was opened in 1886 by the National Telephone Company. These women were telephonists in the early years of the twentieth century. They are thought to be, from left to right: Susi Pearce, -?-, Margery Richardson, Susan Towille.

Opposite below: Miss Quinn and Miss Topman are in close-up here. The first subscriber to the telephone service in York was Doctor Tempest Anderson and in 1886 there were just eleven subscribers. In 1892 the Post Office opened a rival exchange in Lendal and by this time competition was keen, as there were 113 subscribers in the city.

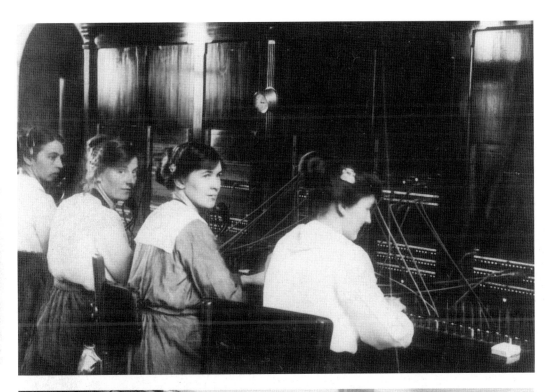

Above: These stonemasons are almost certainly working on the restoration of the central tower of the minster, which took place in the 1920s. The man at the rear is probably Fred Smith, who was a mason at this time.

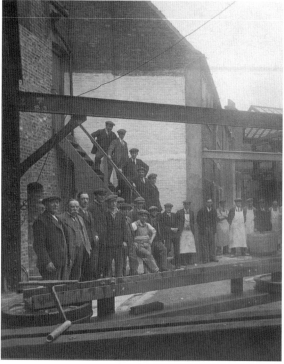

Left: The full complement of workers in the minster stone yard are pictured here in the 1920s. By this time the yard had been moved to its current location on Deangate; previously it had been on the site that the Purey Cust Hospital currently occupies.

Above and left: A new pinnacle, probably for the central tower, is being worked on by a mason and the results examined by Mr Charles Green, Clerk of the Works. These are press photographs and were probably taken just before the pinnacle was hoisted into place.

Left: This gentleman was a member of the oldest police force in the country, the Minster Police, and was photographed in around 1900. The police date back to the thirteenth century, although they were not formally founded until 1829. For many years the minster also had its own prison to punish miscreants whose crimes had taken place within the Minster Close.

Below: The minster also had its own fire brigade and they are pictured here in around 1950. The man on the left is Charles Green, son of the previously pictured Charles Green, and on the far right is W. Jesse Green, who was Clerk of the Works.

This scholar is undertaking research in the minster library in the 1860s. The library was originally built as the private chapel of the Archbishop's palace, which was built for Archbishop Walter de Gray in around 1230 but fell into disuse in the sixteenth century and eventually became derelict. In around 1810 it was restored to become the minster library. The original library was started as early as AD 778, but these works did not survive the Viking raids or Norman Conquest so the earliest records in the collection are those of the Dean and Chapter's own archive, which date from 1150 onwards. The earliest books to survive are from 1414 and the library now holds about 120,000 books, pamphlets and rare documents.

Above left: This unnamed gentleman was the mace bearer to the Merchant Adventurer's Guild in 1907. In earlier times the mace would have been made of wood and its original function was to create a path through a crowd for dignitaries of the Guild.

Above right: This equally smart but rather less intense-looking young man was a footman to the Lord Mayor in 1905. His staff also only had a ceremonial function.

Left: Sir Joseph Terry (seen here in around 1890) was born in 1828, the son of the founder of Joseph Terry and Co. and educated at St Peter's School. He led an illustrious civic life, being made a Freeman in 1850, Lord Mayor four times and sheriff in 1870. He was made an alderman in 1874 and knighted in 1887.

Albert Moore was a York-born painter most well known for his paintings of harmoniously draped young women in the Pre-Raphaelite style. He was one of the more famous Victorian painters but lived a retired life in Holland Park in London. He died from cancer in 1893 – this picture was probably taken not long before he passed away.

Some of the nurses and patients at the Yearsley Bridge Infectious Diseases Hospital are pictured here in around 1910. The beds in the individual huts behind were designed to serve the dual purposes of isolating the patient and exposing them to vast amounts of fresh air, which was considered particularly important for cases of tuberculosis and other lung complaints.

Opposite above: The young boys shown outside this open ward may have been treated for polio. A child's life in hospital at this time would seem shocking to us today – family were often not allowed to visit and a child with an illness such as TB may not have seen their parents for months.

Opposite below: The staff of the public library are pictured here in around 1905. They are, from right to left: Mr Furnish, Mr F. Bewlay, Mr L. Huntley, Mr A. Finney, Mr I. Newbold, Mr S.M. Bryant, Mr I. Oliver, Mr A.E. Freeston, Mr H. Arnott and Mr I. Smith. Arthur H. Furnish was the first city librarian and earned £170 a year; his assistant was paid £70.

Above: Flooding is as much a part of York's history as racing, chocolate and trains – perhaps more so because it can always be relied upon. This soldier is punting a boat carrying stranded people from the Salisbury Road and Leeman Road area during the floods on 29 December 1978. Recent improvements in flood defences have protected many of the areas of the city but others remain vulnerable.

Opposite: This is Arthur Hemmens, one of York's characters, who for many years had a grocer's shop on North Street. Mr Hemmens had a large collection of valuable old prints and rare books which he left to the city and the library when he died in 1944, aged ninety-four. A venerable old man, he remembered the soldiers returning from the Crimean War and watched the parade that marked the arrival in York of the cannon that were captured at Sebastopol. He also remembered the days when Ouse Bridge was the only way across the river other than by ferry. He came to York when he was six months old, at which time the shop belonged to his aunt. Although North Street has always been vulnerable to flooding Mr Hemmens only remembered his shop flooding once, in the Great Flood of 1892, when he had a foot of water in his kitchen. He recalled people in the courts on the Ouse side of North Street being cut off entirely; one group of drinking men ended up having to wade out, having taken no notice of the warnings they were given. Narrow pleasure boats were rowed down the passages to get supplies to people trapped on upper floors.

A group of soldiers are sandbagging at the water purification works during the 1947 flood. In York's long history of flooding the Army has often been called upon to help with building temporary flood defences.

These men are trying to save what possessions they can from houses on Beech Avenue, which were flooded by Holgate Beck during the same flood. The area around Holgate Beck has shown signs of Neolithic settlement but it has only recently been defended against flooding.

A crowd is watching the rescue of some young women during the flood, although they look less than concerned by their predicament. The 1947 flood was the worst the city had experienced since 1831 and the levels were not much less than those experienced by the city in November 2000, when the Ouse reached its highest levels since records began. In 1947 there was an exceptional fall of snow in the hills during the first quarter of the year and then a sudden thaw, during which all of the accumulated water ran off into the rivers. This combined with high seasonal tides and caused chaos, not just in York but across the rest of the country.

Left: William Pumphrey (1817–1905) was a Quaker science teacher and an enthusiastic photographer. He bought his licence from Samuel Walker, York's first practising photographer, in July 1849 and ran his business in the city until 1854. In 1866 he organised an exhibition of 'Yorkshire Fine Art and Industry' in which he entered two revolving stereoscopes, each containing fifty of his views.

Below: Pumphrey took this view of the prison governor's house and Clifford's Tower in 1853. The deer on the Eye of York is transparent because of the necessary length of the exposure.

George Fowler Jones was an architect who used photography to record his buildings for over fifty years. He established an architectural practice in York in 1846, being responsible for many well-known buildings in the city, including Clifton church, and for restoration work on the Red Tower. His earliest pictures are from 1851, making him York's first known amateur photographer.

Jones designed the gatehouse for the Museum Gardens and probably also took this picture, as he often recorded his buildings photographically. He designed the gatehouse in 1874 and it has since been described as 'an engaging piece of Victorian nonsense'.

Above right: Arnold Rowntree was born into the famous Rowntree family in 1872. A member of the Liberal Party, he was elected MP for York in 1910. He was opposed to Britain's involvement in the First World War and in 1914 helped form the Union of Democratic Control (UDC), which became the leading anti-war organisation in Britain.

Above left: His wife, Mary Katherine Rowntree, is pictured during her husband's time as sheriff, 1931-32. Mary and Arnold wrote long letters to each other throughout any time they were forced to be apart. This was particularly true during the First World War, when Arnold struggled with his joint commitments as a pacifist and an MP.

Henry Isaac Rowntree was, along with all the Rowntrees, a strong supporter of the Adult School movement. Henry launched a coffee cart scheme in 1871, which sold coffee as an alternative to alcohol for the young men working at the markets. The first cart was built by George Pattinson.

York's adult schools were immensely popular with both men and women. This is Mary Olivia Kitching, who was president of the 'B' class at Lady Peckitt's Yard Women's School. She worked and taught there for fourteen years before leaving for the Holy Land to undertake missionary work in 1892.

Above and below: These small dancers are some of the pupils at New Earswick school in 1918. The school was officially opened by Joseph Rowntree in the winter of 1912. He used his opening speech to emphasise some of his ideas on education. He believed in the importance of co-education from infants up; that success depended upon high-quality teachers, but that a well-planned building would help them to be effective; that girls should be allowed equality of opportunity; that the object was not merely to instill facts but to teach children how to discover them; that success was judged by how far the school produced good men and women; and that school life should not be cut short by the need to go to work.

These advanced ideas regarding the education of girls are illustrated in the science room in 1917. The children are Edith Neal, Doris Powell, Cyril Charlton and John Skelton. The school was largely an open-air building, with windows that folded back on its south side. The sills were low so that the children could see out of the windows from their desks.

The boys are alone in their pursuit of woodwork because girls would have been engaged in learning domestic pursuits – equality of opportunity only went so far in a world where men and women still moved within very separate spheres.

The Folk Hall in New Earswick was used for worship and as a meeting place. This is the Girls Club, where the young women are engaged in a variety of occupations including knitting and practising first aid. Many clubs were dominated by activities geared towards the support of the troops engaged in the war.

These are the boys of the York Minster Song School in around 1909. The master on the right is Dr Thomas Tertius Noble, who was the minster's organist between 1897 and 1913. The man on the left is possibly the headmaster, George Arthur Scaife. The boy second left on the back row is probably W. Jesse Green, who later became the Clerk of Works of the minster.

three

War and
Peace

These are the officers of the 14th Regimental District, York in September 1886. They are, from left to right, back row (standing): Captain Seymour, 3rd Yorkshire Regiment; Quartermaster Pye, 3rd West Yorkshire Regiment; Quartermaster Croft, 3rd Yorkshire Regiment; Captain St George, 2nd West Yorkshire Regiment. Middle row (sitting): Major Pigott, 1st West Yorkshire Regiment; Colonel Phillips,

Commander 14th Regimental District; an unknown child (Colonel Phillips' son?); Major Morris, 1st West Yorkshire Regiment; Captain Bayley, 4th West Yorkshire Regiment. Front row (lying): Lieutenant Swaine, Adjutant 14th Regimental District; Major McGachen, Staff Pay Master 14th Regimental District.

Soldiers and civilians are on Castle Mills Bridge, almost certainly in 1899 at the start of the Boer War. A later photograph shows Lord Roberts passing over the same bridge. The 1909 pageant was to include a little-known bugler who was taking part in the Civil War re-enactment. He was Corporal Shurlock of the 5th Royal Irish Lancers, and he had sounded the first cavalry charge of the Boer War.

This gun, known as the 'Boer War Gun', was kept near the Green Howards Monument on Tower Street. It was a facsimile used for competitions and training in gun manoeuvring. The Anglo-Boer War of 1899 was one of the most bitter struggles of the Victorian age – it involved scores of regiments of the regular British Army, as well as Yeomanry and other volunteer regiments. York suffered what were considered to be significant casualties and a memorial was erected in Duncombe Place to commemorate the South African war dead.

Left and below: The unveiling of the South African War Memorial took place in Duncombe Place on 3 August 1905. Dignitaries, including Lord Roberts, arrived at the site from Mansion House. Lieutenant General Sir Leslie Rundle and a member of his staff are also pictured. Crowds are gathered on the ubiquitous scaffolding on the minster, although the numbers of people who gathered at the ceremony were considered modest. This was mainly due to persistent rain, although the half-hour delay due to luncheon and toasts at Mansion House over-running probably didn't help.

Above and left: The crowds on Blake Street and in St Helen's Square are watching the parade for Military Sunday in 1907. This proud York tradition was started in 1885 as a memorial to General Gordon, who was killed at Khartoum. Military Sunday continued unchecked through the First World War but was ended by the world-shattering events of 1939. The large Harker's York Hotel is on the current site of the world famous Betty's Café Tearooms.

This is the Junior Commanders School at Strensall Camp during the First World War. The photograph is from an album belonging to a Miss Hodgkinson, who lived at The Lodge in Strensall at this time. She knew a large number of officers and may have done some nursing.

These soldiers are from the York and Lancashire Regiment and were probably pictured at Strensall. The soldier on the left (marked with a cross) was Major Robertson, who was killed in the First World War, probably in 1915. The soldier in the middle (marked) is Colonel Daniell. The last indicated soldier is Captain East, who was also killed in 1915.

messrs. Freedman + angus

These soldiers leaning nonchalantly in the doorway of The Lodge in Strensall are named by the photographer as 'Messers Freedman and Angus'. Miss Hodgkinson's album is both a sad and an evocative document, filled as it is with photographs of young men who were later to die. It appears that this pair, however, made it safely through the conflict.

These soldiers are at Strensall Camp during the First World War. The soldier in the foreground is thought to be Lieutenant Kinder of the West Yorkshire Leeds Rifles. The Leeds Rifles were formed in Carlton Barracks in 1914.

Above: This group of Army bandsmen are pictured at Strensall Camp in 1914. The sergeant is thought to be a Sergeant A. Helps.

Right: This postcard is part of a moving series which were produced during the First World War showing the men of each area who were killed in action. These are the servicemen of the Fulford Road district. The photographs were produced in a size and shape which made them suitable for wearing in a locket.

William Varley, sitting on the left, was a conscientious objector from Chestnut Grove in New Earswick. He was called up on 18 October 1916 but refused to follow orders, leading to a tribunal to assess his CO status. He was held in Wormwood Scrubs and eventually accepted 'Work of National Importance'. Varley has written on the back that these are the 'stoking staff'. He sent a postcard to his wife from prison at Christmas 1917 in which he wrote 'May our "little bit" of prison separation do something towards an everlasting Peace on Earth... Not forgetting the boys still suffering.' He also wrote to his mother that he hoped 'the scheme soon goes bust'.

Opposite above: The purpose of this assembly in the grounds of the Purey Cust Nursing Home is unclear, although it is probably part of the peace celebrations that were held in August 1919. During the war the hospital had been used to nurse soldiers, although they do not seem particularly well represented at the party, most presumably having returned to civilian life.

Opposite below: The civic procession leaves the war memorial after its unveiling in 1925. The memorial was erected on ground given by the North Eastern Railway Company in 1923 which had previously been an exercise area for horses. The Gardens of Remembrance were opened by the Duke and Duchess of York, later King George VI and Queen Elizabeth.

York had eleven air raids during the Second World War, with the Baedeker Raid of April 1942 being the worst. Over 7,600 homes were damaged in the raid and seventeen 'rest centres' fed and accommodated over 2,000 homeless people. Eighty-seven civilians were killed and 205 injured.

Members of a Civil Defence Group are pictured in the Museum Gardens. Over twenty planes took part in the Baedeker Raid and the civil defence teams pulled eighty-nine people from ruined buildings, thirty-seven of whom were rescued alive. Four Civil Defence workers and a member of the National Fire Service were also killed.

The Guildhall, burning during the raid. There were fifty-eight fires caused by incendiary bombs – nine of them designated 'serious' at the time. Four first aid posts dealt with seventy-four cases and 1,104 Civil Defence workers turned out. The Clifton first aid post continued to provide help after having its windows blown out and its water heater damaged.

The bombs began dropping almost simultaneously with the sirens sounding so there was, in effect, no warning. This was a concentrated attack lasting for around an hour with sixty-nine high explosive bombs and a large number of incendiary bombs. The bombs hit Coney Street, the Guildhall, Rowntree's warehouse, the station, Bootham, Clifton, Leeman Road, Poppleton Road and Burton Stone Lane.

The Bar Convent was hit and five nuns killed – these men are beginning the terrible task of clearing the rubble. The raid made many people homeless and the Lord Mayor set up a relief fund. An 'all star variety concert' with Alaister Sim was held at the Rialto and a charitable auction included paper doileys, a bottle of lemonade, a moustache cup and a Maltese lace collar.

On the second anniversary of the Baedeker Raid civic leaders and civil defence officials gathered around this 1,100lb high explosive bomb in the shell of the Guildhall. The city received the bomb from the Civil Defence, who had used it to collect £60 for air raid victims as a sign of defiance.

The damage to St Martin Le Grand church can be seen clearly in the distance. The papers were full of 'uplifting' stories in an attempt to counter the great shock felt by the citizens of the city at their losses. These included the story of a pair of swans who remained on their nest despite a bomb falling only 20ft away. They were unhurt.

These are probably the peace celebrations at Monk Bar at the end of the Second World War. This portcullis is the last working one in the city and it had been lowered in 1914 for the first time in 300 years.

four

Worship and
Celebration

These dapper gentlemen are by the minster in around 1865. The massive building behind them is the old deanery, which was replaced by a new building in Minster Place and demolished in 1938. The deanery was designed by J.P. Pritchett in a Tudor style and built between 1827 and 1831 – at the time it was very up-to-date, as it had a hot water system.

Above: This bell ringer, in the ringing chamber of the minster, is pictured in around 1900. The bells were originally housed in the central tower but it collapsed in 1407 and architects believed that the weight of the bells may have played a part in weakening the structure. The bells were moved to the west nave, with two towers being built to house them.

Left: This view towards the minster across the rooftops from the top of Monk Bar has been very much photographed. On this occasion (*c.* 1865) the photographer is unknown.

These boys are in front of St Sampson's church on Church Street (*c.* 1890). St Sampson's was originally a medieval church in the centre of the city. At the time Church Street was known as 'Girdlergate' – the street of belt makers. In 1968 it closed its doors because of a dwindling city centre population.

The board over the door of the Holy Trinity church on Micklegate names those who held office in the parish at this time (around 1885). G.W. Umpleby and Adolphus Graves were the churchwardens, Thomas Rutter and William Tate were the overseers and C.H. Russell was the guardian. This pictured group may well be these named men.

This is the wedding of Miss Nancy Lycett Green (daughter of Sir Edward Lycett Green) and Captain Adrian Rose on 7 December 1907. The guard of honour were formed by the Royal Horse Guards. Tragically Captain Rose died on 25 March 1908, aged only twenty-nine.

The Archbishop, William Temple, and the Dean are pictured welcoming in the New Year outside the minster at midnight on 31 December 1929. Archbishop Temple was newly ordained. He became Archbishop of Canterbury in 1944.

A children's fête was held to celebrate Queen Victoria's Diamond Jubilee on 22 June 1897. York held a variety of events, including a 'Tea to 1,200 Aged and Necessitous Poor' and a 'Procession of the Corporation, Magistrates, Clergy, etc, etc.' The Royal English Circus gave a 'Grand Fashionable Performance' and there was a breakfast and a gala.

The Princess Henry of Battenberg (Beatrice, the youngest daughter of Queen Victoria) visited the city on 24 October 1905. Her main duty was to unveil a statue of her mother in the Guildhall. She was accompanied by her daughter, Victoria Eugenie. The statue of Queen Victoria now stands in West Bank Park in Acomb.

The civic party are pictured on the steps of the minster for the Proclamation of King George V on 10 May 1910. Town Clerk Henry Craven is reading the proclamation. Behind him the two men with chains of office are the Lord Mayor James Birch and Sheriff William A. Forster-Todd.

Edward, the Prince of Wales, is inspecting the ex-servicemen in the Mansion House Yard on his way down to the Guildhall for the presentation of the Honorary Freedom of the City on 31 May 1923. The Chief Constable of York, Henry Woolnough Esq. can be seen on the left in the background in a black uniform.

DECORATED REGENT ST DURING JUBILEE CELEBRATION WEEK 1935.

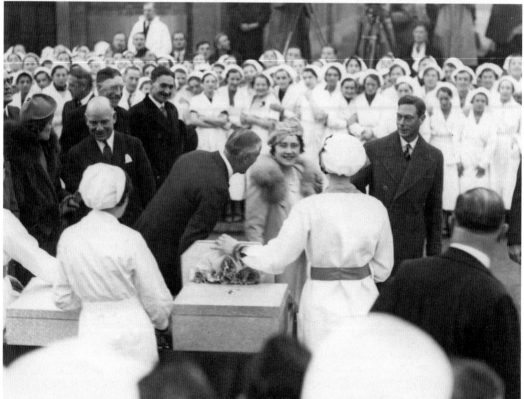

Above: HRH Queen Elizabeth is talking to the Lord Mayor, Thomas Morris, on Tuesday 19 October 1937. The Princess Royal, Lord Harewood and the General Officer Commanding in Chief, Northern Command, are looking on. The King was inspecting the guard of honour outside Terry's Café at this point. A contemporary newspaper described how the red carpet outside Mansion House became untidy because it had been knocked by cars dropping people off, so a little girl in the crowd ran across to straighten it for the royal couple.

Opposite above: Regent Street is decorated for the Silver Jubilee of George V and Queen Mary in May 1935. George V started the annual Christmas broadcast by the sovereign to the Empire (more recently to the Commonwealth), the first being transmitted in 1932 by the relatively new medium of radio.

Opposite below: George VI and Elizabeth visited the works of Joseph Terry on 19 October 1937. They over-stayed their visit and apparently enjoyed hearing that the girls in the packing department sang for half an hour each morning and afternoon. The Queen is being presented with an 8lb box of chocolates bearing the York coat of arms by Miss Beatrice Weaver.

The Queen is walking down Museum Street, with the Lord Mayor, Alderman Richard Scruton, in 1971. There were large crowds, particularly at the Lendal end of Museum Street, and nearly seventy schoolchildren had to be passed over the heads of the crowds to the first aid point to avoid being crushed by the crowds. The first aid point also rescued two poodles.

The Queen's coach is followed by an escort from the 1st Division of Life Guards. Street lining was provided by units of the Army and RAF. The crowd was described in a contemporary report: 'over half were schoolchildren. The rest [were] mostly mothers, taking time off from cooking teas – and a few fathers, home early from work.'

This appears to be a sale of work or bazaar and is probably in aid of the Lawrence Street Sunday school (*c.* 1890). Bazaars were an immensely popular way to raise funds at this time and women took great pride in the small handicrafts they produced for their stall.

'Demon drink' was seen by some as the worst social evil faced by Victorian society and many attempts were made to make a life without alcohol seem as acceptable, if not more so, than the alternative. These children are attending the St Lawrence's Temperance Treat in July 1893.

York has long been a cycling city and for some years there was a fashion for entering decorated bicycles in parades. This young woman is ready to take part in the York Lifeboat Saturday procession on 8 July 1899.

86

Left: These two women are attending the International Sheepdog Trials on the Knavesmire in September 1923. The York Knavesmire Committee were anxious to make a success of the event, as they had ambitions to host it every year instead of once every three years.

Below: The Duchess of Hamilton and Brandon (shown here with her daughter, Lady Margaret) was supposed to be presenting the prizes at the trials. Unfortunately she was called away on the second day as her son had been involved in an accident, and Lady Margaret presented the prizes instead.

These trumpeters are outside the assize court in around 1910, ready to lead the ceremonial processions which formed part of the pomp surrounding the judging circuit. Assize courts dealt with a wide variety of criminal and civil cases such as murder, arson, riot, counterfeiting coins and sheep stealing.

On this particular occasion the coach contains the High Sheriff of Yorkshire, who rejoiced in the name Frederick James Osbaldiston Montagu. He was probably on his way to the minster as assize sessions always began with a special service there.

The Lord Mayor, Charles William Shipley, is handing a wallet of notes to George Kirby in recognition of his fifty years as curator of the art gallery on 6 May 1930. He would have been eighty-five in the photograph. The man to the left is J.B. Morrell, who was chairman of the Art Gallery Committee, and the magnificently dressed woman is Mrs Shipley.

J.B. Morrell, Captain Ormsby and Major-General Whitfield are inspecting the troops on the occasion of a civic trip to America in 1950. J.B. Morrell took a replica chain as the original, 347 years old and valued at £4,325, was far too valuable to leave the country. He also left behind his robes and hat to keep his luggage weight down!

These are members of the Terry family, probably photographed during the company's anniversary in 1927. Joseph Terry had originally leased a riverside site at Clementhorpe to house his stocks of peel. The riverside location was important as all supplies of sugar, cocoa, glucose, orange and lemon rinds in brine arrived by steam (along with coal supplies) on the river.

Rowntree's Cocoa Works was the first stop on the royal visit of May 1923. The group of directors are posing here after the visit. From left to right: J.S. Rowntree, B.S. Rowntree, Joseph Rowntree, Arnold S. Rowntree, Oscar F. Rowntree.

These are some of the judges from the flower show of June 1925. Categories were very precise, with the 'cut rose' category having seven sub-categories, ranging from '72 Roses From Not Less Than 36 Varieties' through '24 Distinct Varieties' to '12 Single Blooms for Amateurs'.

Coney Street is decorated for Civic Week in June 1928. Coney Street was on the route for the military procession on Military Sunday and the pageant procession. The decorations gave the fire brigade an extra drill (they were doing demonstrations all week anyway) when sparks from the tram-wires on Bridge Street set them alight. Luckily not much damage was done.

Civic Week was a festival to foster and celebrate pride in the city. The attractions included military shows, band performances, tours of municipal services, exhibitions, displays, processions and the incorporation of several yearly events, such as the flower show and gala, Military Sunday and the York Regatta. The latter was used to give a fitting end to the celebrations. This woman is admiring the entries in the 'Hand baskets and Bowls' section of the 66th Annual Flower Show and Gala.

Opposite: These displays of Greek dancing and gymnastics are providing part of the physical training and dancing display held at Rowntree's during the celebrations. There were a series of days where York companies opened their doors to the public, which were considered a great success. A Trades and Industries Exhibition was held in the Assembly Rooms during the same week. Exhibitors included Rowntree's, Terry', Ben Johnson's, the York Gas Company, Adams' Hydraulics, Whitby Oliver and the Rolyat Patent Domestic Hot Water System Company Limited.

This crowd is waiting in Museum Street to see the Pageant Procession which took spectators back through York's history from 'Prehistoric Times' to 'The Coming of the Railways'. These processions were held on the Monday, Wednesday and Friday of Civic Week with the crowds lining the route from Dean's Park, zigzagging through the city centre and ending in the Museum Gardens. Each episode in history was applauded by the onlookers, with a large crowd attending the final episode, re-enacted in the Museum Gardens.

Rowntree's prize-winning brass band is pictured here on the company's Rose Lawn during the Trades and Industries Exhibition. A Grand Military Display was held and the programme included a musical ride performed by the 14th/20th Hussars, the trooping of French drums captured in the Peninsular War, riding without saddles, standing while riding and jumping over groups of men and dining tables.

A smiling Dick Turpin is bound securely by ropes and has an armed escort. He is being taken to execution as part of the re-enactments of York's history during Civic Week. Mr Turpin is played by R.V. Rodgers, and his captors by serving police officers: T. Richmond, T. Pickering, B. Pickering and N. Knowles. 'Black Bess' is being held by F. Metcalfe.

York Municipal Aerodrome was opened on 4 July 1936 by Lord Swinton, the Minister for Air, who flew from London in an RAF machine and had lunch at Mansion House. The Lord Mayor presided over the ceremony and Lord Swinton, seen speaking here, presented him with the licence, receiving a silver cigarette box in return.

Lady Helmsley is leaving the All Saints church Sunday school Bazaar in Upper Poppleton after fulfilling her duty in opening it on 5 July 1910. Lady Helmsley's sister was Lady Theresa Castlereagh.

These children are gathered on the recreation field on Leeman Road for the Burton Lane Adult School Children's Carnival of 1908. Carnivals, sales of work and games tournaments were often held to raise funds for good causes and the work of the adult schools.

In 1907 the York Adult Schools celebrated their jubilee. Here residents of Hungate have decorated their street – many will have been members of the school. Adult Schools began with the ideal that learning could and should be available to all – an advertisement from the time adjures members to 'come as you are, do not stop to black your boots'.

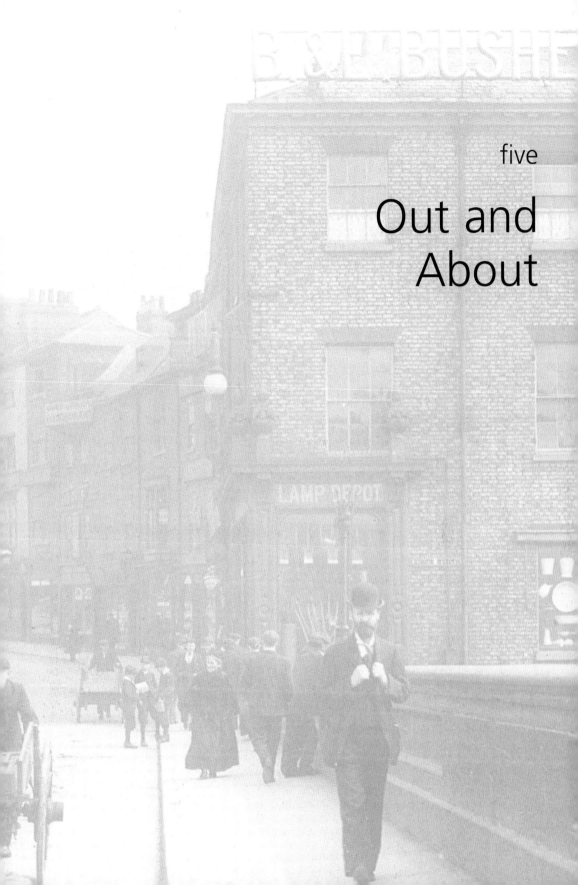

five

Out and
About

Lancashire v Yorkshire Air Race 2nd Oct 1913.

The Lancashire and Yorkshire Air Race took place on 2 October 1913. Mr A.V. Roe and his biplane, built in Lancashire and piloted by F.P. Raynham, are pictured on the Knavesmire at the York stopover. The race, known as the 'War of the Roses', was over a 100-mile circuit between the Avro biplane and a Blackburn monoplane piloted by Mr Harold Blackburn, who was from Leeds. This plane has been added to the top left-hand side of the print. The two planes took off at 2.15 p.m. from Moortown and were only a minute apart at York until Mr Blackburn's take-off was hampered by a terrier chasing the wheels of his plane! Mr Blackburn made up the time and went on to win when his opponent failed to find the control point at Barnsley.

Opposite above: These children are playing near a Handley Page W8 Airliner on the Knavesmire, probably in the late 1920s. The W8 was the mainstay of the Imperial Airways fleet until 1927 and was operated from London Airport at Croydon.

Opposite below: Monsieur Salmet and his 80hp Blériot monoplane are pictured on the Knavesmire in 1913 during the *Daily Mail* aeroplane tour. Henri Salmet was the chief instructor of the Blériot Company's flying school at Hendon.

Mr R. Reeder is standing by a Gypsy II Moth G-AFKY. The Moths belonging to York Flying Club were pressed into service after the Munich Crisis as part of the Civil Air Guard. The three or four owned by the Yorkshire Air Service were utilised to train pilots, which freed up service pilots for the front line in the event of war.

Harold Sydney Reeder is pictured with an Avro cadet, one of seven aircraft owned by the air club at York. The fleet included a Hornet, Gypsy Moths and Leopard Moths. After consideration of Hob Moor, Copmanthorpe and Heslington, the 163-acre site at Clifton was chosen because it was surrounded by meadows suitable for use as an air circus.

Decorated trams are travelling down Tower Street on 20 January 1910, the first day that electric trams ran in York. The first car, No. 1, left the depot at noon driven by the Lord Mayor, Alderman James Birch, and driver J.A. Stewart, followed by five other cars. During this first day 6,786 passengers were carried and receipts were £35 18s 5d.

The trams are pictured at their depot at Fulford Cross on 14 September 1911. A city report from the time says that conductors on the trams would get 22 shillings for a sixty-hour week, increasing to a maximum of 25 shillings. They were also allowed seven days a year paid holiday.

Left: This engine is being given oil in the York North Motive Power Depot (Engine Shed), which originally had four turntables. Sections of its walls still exist but have been incorporated into other buildings as part of the National Railway Museum.

Below: York City trolleybus No. 30 (registration VY 2991) is passing No. 115 East Parade on its way out of town. Second Avenue is off to the bottom left. The trolleybus network in York consisted of only one route. It opened in 1920 and closed in 1935.

This Corporation steamroller is trundling west along Lawrence Street in around 1890, with the tower of the old St Lawrence church in the background. This church was usurped by a much bigger one with a spire in 1881, but the tower remains as an ancient relic of Lawrence Street from before it was changed forever by the siege of 1644.

Micklegate Bar and Blossom Street, probably in the mid-1920s. Traditionally the reigning monarch enters the city through Micklegate Bar – previously the main route into the city from the south – but must first ask permission to enter the walled city.

These children are in a pony cart, probably on Lawrence Street, in the mid-1890s. This would never have been considered an elegant vehicle.

Members of the No. 17 District Conservative Party are gathered on Lawrence Street, outside the Tam O'Shanter Hotel, for a drive round Buttercrambe Woods in June 1901.

The charabancs have reached the woods, which would have been a round trip of around twenty-five miles. The waggonettes were supplied by John Burland of Fetter Lane.

The York and District butcher's excursion to Loch Lomond was on 25 June 1909. All the members of the excursion are carefully dressed in suits and hats and many are also carrying overcoats, which suggests that the weather may not have been kind to them.

This civic group, in a picture which probably dates from the 1930s, is at an unidentified location. Presumably the trip has a pleasure element as the older man on the right of the group has a camera round his neck as well as a box brownie in his hand.

These are the Rowntree children on their annual holiday on the North York Moors (*c.* 1920). From the shortest: Mary Crosfield, Richard Rowntree, Priscilla Crosfield, Anna Crosfield, Michael Rowntree, Mary Rowntree, Derek Crosfield, Betty Ford, Margaret Rowntree and Tessa Rowntree.

This view across St Sampson's Square towards Parliament Street probably dates from around 1905. Excavations here found a Roman caldarium, or bath, and many artefacts, the most interesting probably being footprints in the tiles. One of the tiles holds an indentation of the insignia of the 9th Legion, the founders of Eboracum in AD 71.

Opposite above: The square is pictured here between 1955 and 1958, well before pedestrianisation. On the left the Golden Lion Hotel and the Dukes Bros fish restaurant are both now part of Browns. Henry Ward's tool shop was an old-fashioned place where you could buy tools for all trades from staff who were happy to sell a single washer.

Opposite below: Parliament Street, busy on a market day in 1961. The market was created by an Act of Parliament in 1833 in order to ease congestion on Pavement, and the first market was held here in June 1836. The ancient market was spread out, with different parts of the street holding different kinds of goods.

Above: Close examination of this scene, taken from Micklegate Bar looking down Micklegate in around 1890, shows that the people are all carefully dressed and heading in the same direction. It is only possible to speculate but the crowd may have been attending a parade or other event.

Left: This shop on Stonegate, which dates from around 1434, was opened as the 'Eclectic Bookshop' by Thomas Charles Godfrey in 1895. Mr Godfrey controversially claimed to be a 'professor' of phrenology, holding consultations in rooms on Gillygate. Phrenology suggested that people's head size and shape indicated their personality and Mr Godfrey travelled widely measuring people's heads in pursuit of his 'science'.

Opposite below: These people are on Swinegate in the late 1890s. Swinegate was known in Viking and medieval times as Swinegail, meaning the lane where swine were kept. Gate in this context means 'street' rather than the gates into the city which are, rather confusingly, referred to as 'bars'.

Above: This end of Jubbergate was originally known as High Jubbergate and the group are standing in front of Mr A. Well's brokering premises in around 1880. This medieval building is reputed to have housed six families at this time. Forrington's furniture dealers moved in in around 1920 and the building has since been occupied by a succession of cafés and eateries.

Above: 'The Doss House' at 111 Walmgate is shown in the autumn of 1913. This half-timbered fifteenth-century building was for many years a common lodging house run by the Kilmartin family. The advertisements invite the reader to a series of lectures on local history by Dr W.A. Evelyn in the Tempest Anderson Hall. A football match is advertised between York City and Newcastle United at Field View, which was situated at the end of Burton Stone Lane, on Wednesday 15 October. The Rugby League has a match between York and Runcorn.

Opposite above: 'The Doss House' is pictured here in a somewhat happier state, although the sign for 'Good lodgings down this passage' was, by all accounts, rather exaggerated. Ebor Court, also signed, contained ten small houses. In 1961 the building was acquired by the Civic Trust, restored and named Bowes Morrell House in memory of J.B. Morrell, a founding member of the Trust.

Opposite below: The junction of Tanner's Moat, Rougier Street and Museum Street is pictured in around 1955. The unusually shaped three-storey building had previously been Walker's Horse Repository (and incidentally named as the ugliest building in Europe). Later it became a car dealers and lost its top storey.

114

Tanner's Moat had been occupied by some of the most famous names in York's industrial heritage – Rowntree's had used a warehouse here until it was destroyed in the Second World War, and the typewriter dealers had previously been occupied by John Smith's brewery offices.

Opposite above: This vast gate was one of the entrances to the prison complex which was centred around Clifford's Tower. It is pictured here in around 1910 from the inside – the walls of Clifford's Tower are to the right of the frame. The buildings surrounding the castle, including this gatehouse (with two towers for lodging the porters and turnkeys), were constructed in 1835.

Opposite below: The prison was demolished 100 years later in 1935, when this picture was taken. In 1900 the male prison had been made available to the War Office as a military prison, which closed in 1929 and ceased to be a prison at all in 1932. The sign on the right-hand tower advertises building materials from the demolition for sale.

562-26   THE CASTLE GATE, YORK.

DRIVE
SLOWLY

DEAD SLOW

TIMBER
BRICKS
FLAGS
& STONE
FOR SALE

Coney Street was photographed by the City Engineers at 10.35 a.m. on 7 June 1980 as part of the records required for pedestrianisation. The city now has one of the largest pedestrianised areas in Europe.

High Petergate is shown at 4.20 p.m. on 12 June 1980. The Minerva (Goddess of Wisdom) figure on the corner was carved by Francis Wolstenholme of Gillygate. He was the cousin of shop owner John Wolstenholme, who published the first *Yorkshire Gazette* in April 1819. Minerva signifies that the shop sold books, but lottery tickets and medicines were also available.

Davygate is pictured at 10.15 a.m. on 5 June 1980 before the pedestrianisation of this area, so there are a significant number of delivery vans and St Sampson's Square is still a car park. To the right is 'Brown's corner'. Brown's department store was founded by Henry Rhodes Brown in 1891 and moved to its present site in 1900.

Davygate (10.40 a.m. on 5 June 1980) is the home of the famous Betty's Café Tea Rooms. These are still managed and owned by descendents of Frederick Belmont, a Swiss confectioner who ended up in Yorkshire because, unable to speak English, he boarded the wrong train on his arrival in London at the turn of the twentieth century.

King's Square was the site of Christ Church (or Holy Trinity) which was demolished in 1937, leaving a raised area much used as an impromptu stage by street entertainers.

This 1955 view shows the final stages of the creation of Stonebow. The site was originally occupied by houses of the Hungate area, which were demolished in around 1935. On the left is Russell's garage, founded in 1945, which was to expand to the other side of the road and have a life of over fifty years.

The corner of New Street and Davygate was damaged during the air raids of the Second World War and the buildings were demolished. The area was not rebuilt until the mid-1950s and this view is almost unrecognisable today. The picture probably dates from around 1949.

These women are at the side of the Theatre Royal in St Leonard's Place, probably in the mid-1950s. In 1967 a glass and concrete wing was added to this north wall.

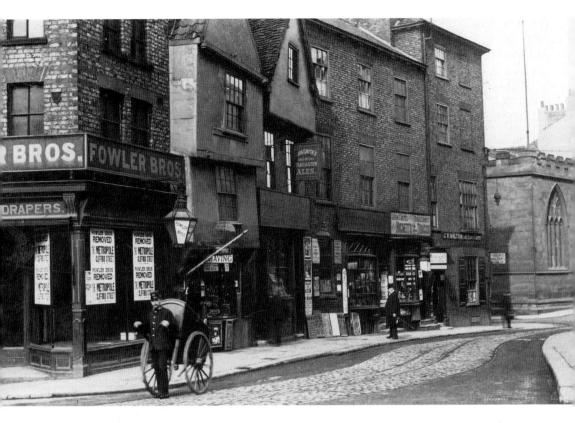

It is unclear why the gentleman in the foreground of this 1890s scene on Nessgate is wearing a uniform but he is probably a postman or may be a porter. Some of these premises were demolished in 1903 to widen Nessgate, including the Star and Garter Inn which is in approximately the centre of the row. In T.P. Cooper's book *The Old Inns and Inn Signs of York* (1897) the entry for the Star and Garter on Nessgate states that the name refers to the insignia of the Order of the Garter. 'The popular and romantic circumstances to the origin of the order are merely traditional. Its foundation is uncertain, but authorities assign its institution to the year 1344, during the reign of Edward III. The Star was added to the insignia by Charles I, in the second year of his reign. The old house shows signs of antiquity, it no doubt was erected anterior to Charles' reign.'

Opposite above: Ouse Bridge (pictured in around 1900) was completed in 1820 to replace a Tudor construction. Until 1863 it was the only structural link between the north and south banks of the Ouse. This version was built alongside the Tudor bridge with its chapel and houses, which had replaced a medieval version which had collapsed. In 1376 this had thirty-six shops, five tenements and one house 'overhanging the river'.

Opposite below: Millfield Lodge on Hull Road is pictured in 1893. At this time it was a property within the grounds of a large residence, Millfield House. The photographer has indicated that one of the men has the initials T.B.

This little girl is standing on Monkgate in the early 1900s. At this time the gasworks were close by and the quality of air in this area could be very poor indeed.

This very damp police officer standing on point duty at the junction of Duncombe Place, Blake Street, St Leonard's Place and Museum Street in around 1925 would have had a very different view not so many years earlier. Before the creation of Duncombe Place the view to the minster was obscured by medieval buildings, which formed Lop Lane.

Before the time of this picture (*c.* 1900) this building on the corner of Davygate and St Sampson's Square had been a potato and fruit merchant for over half a century. For much of the time since, the much altered premises have been occupied by Brown's department store.

The Society of Architect's meeting is here being held at Heslington Hall in around 1870. It is likely that this is specifically the York or North Yorkshire Society. The hall was completed in 1568 for Thomas Eynns, who was the Keeper of the Seal for the Council of the North.

Opposite above: This man is breaking stone between Layerthorpe Bridge and the city walls sometime between 1905 and 1912. The large premises and chimney in the background belong to J.J. Hunt's Ebor Brewery on Aldwark. The yard and premises on the left show signs for Martin Caffrey, a builder who lived at 29 Portland Street between 1905 and 1912.

Opposite below: The man leading the horse on Main Street in Nether Poppleton is thought to be a George or 'Billy' Walker – also known as Billy 'Butcher' Walker – and the young woman at the right of the frame is Grace Dibbs. The pub on the left is the Lord Nelson.

Other local titles published by Tempus

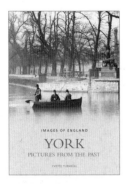

York Pictures from the Past
YVETTE TURNBULL

This fascinating collection of over 200 photographs illustrates the long relationship that photographers have had with this historic city as they have worked to capture its beauty in the past 150 years. Many of the glass plates and lantern slides were previously unknown, and are published here for the first time, accompanied by illuminating captions, anecdotes and local stories.

0 7524 3247 8

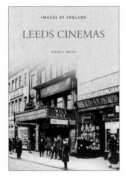

Leeds Cinemas
ROBERT E. PREEDY

With over 200 old photographs, programmes and advertisements, this book provides a fascinating look at the history of cinema-going in the city of Leeds and its suburbs over the last hundred years. It includes chapters on the technology behind the silver screen and the entrepreneurs and cinema chains which operated in the area. The images in this book will delight all those who have fond memories of visiting some of Leeds' picture houses, many of which disappeared long ago.

0 7524 3583 3

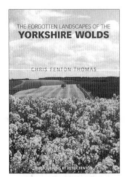

Forgotten landscapes of the Yorkshire Wolds
CHRIS FENTON-THOMAS

The author outlines the changes the Wolds went through and how these contrasted with the surrounding lowlands. He also shows how many aspects of this landscape survived over the centuries. The communities living here held a deep association with the valleys, viewpoints and meres but also with the past that was visible in the landscape around them in the banks and barrows of their ancestors.

0 7524 3346 6

Fighting men of the North
RONNIE WHARTON

The North East of England has been witness to some of the finest fighting men in the boxing world. Featured here are 22 of the greatest over the past 100 years, with full biographies and career statistics. This story covers the first glove champions Will Curley, George Chrisp and Jack Palmer through to present-day fighters such as middleweight Cornelius Carr, a challenger for World honours, and Hartlepool's new and exciting British champion Michael Hunter. Illustrated throughout, this is an essential read for any boxing fan.

0 7524 3551 5

If you are interested in purchasing other books published by Tempus, or in case you have difficulty finding any Tempus books in your local bookshop, you can also place orders directly through our website

www.tempus-publishing.com